Healing With A Smile:

The Story of a Shark Attack

A Grateful Mom and Son

This book is dedicated to everyone who helped.

Table of Contents

Chapter 1: It Happened!

"Your son has been bitten by a shark," I hear when I answer the phone at 9:26 a.m. on Saturday, September 8, 2018. Juliun, my son, was in the ambulance when the paramedic called. The paramedic told me they were on their way to Queen's Hospital, and then he held the phone to Juliun's ear and my son said, "Mom, I'm okay."

I was in the car headed north when I got the call. I remember looking at the incoming number as the phone rang, wondering who was calling as I pulled the car off the road and answered. The call was very short. After hanging up, I remember saying a prayer, a prayer that I never imagined having to say. With the help of Heavenly Father, I then drove over the mountain to the hospital. I don't remember the drive, but somehow I found my way.

How do I write a book about a shark biting my son? The answer to this question is—the best I can. As I recount the details of this event, I cry. It is hard to believe that this happened and even harder to relive these experiences. When I get the frequent feelings that this task is too difficult, I think about all the people who are struggling throughout the world. This is a story about miracles and heroes, and I know that we need to share this story. I have known this since it happened. As a result, I have recorded much of what has happened along the way. Now, my son and I know it's our overwhelming job to share this account with you.

When Juliun and I first started thinking of titles for this book, what first came to mind was *100 Miracles* because there were so many miracles that happened. As a result, I started focusing on and recording each miracle. On September 11 (three days after the attack), our list of miracles had exceeded 100. Since then, I have had many other thoughts come to mind, and when I think about each possible title, I know they are all good choices. However, the title that Juliun chose was, *Healing with a Smile: The Story of a Shark Attack*. This title sums up our journey of miracles.

Having a focus and purpose for writing this story helped me get started. As soon as I jotted down a few ideas and looked at how we could frame our goals, my task became a little easier. I believe it is important to share our focus and purpose with you at the beginning and end of this book in order to remind us all that:

1. God is near.

2. Miracles happen.

3. Heroes are real.

4. When you see someone in need, help them.

5. Be Strong, Calm, and Grateful.

It is our sincere hope that this story will be a comfort and strength to those in need throughout the world. I begin by sharing some shark facts and a little history about us in order to set the stage, and after that, I recount as much detail as I can about this unbelievable experience.

Chapter 2: Shark Facts

The shark that attacked Juliun is believed to have been a 10-12 foot Tiger Shark. This is what the expert said when he came to our home to measure the 15-inch bite on my son's arm and the marks on his surfboard. Before the attack, I had no idea that shark experts come to homes to record everything they can about shark bites. After the shark bit my son, it helped us both to try to understand sharks a bit more. Here are some shark facts from three different sources to educate you about this fascinating creature.

Brian Handwerk of National Geographic states:

Each year there are about 50 to 70 confirmed shark attacks and 5 to 15 shark-attack fatalities around the world. The numbers have risen over the past several decades but not because sharks are more aggressive: Humans have simply taken to coastal waters in increasing numbers.

With all my heart, I wish these numbers were zero. My thoughts and prayers are with each victim and their family.

On June 18, 2019 ABC's *Nightline* reported that "There were 32 unprovoked shark attacks in the US in 2018 almost half of the worldwide total. The chances of being attacked by a shark are roughly one in 11.5 million." Juliun was one of these thirty-two people. According to the United States Census Bureau, there were 327.2 million people in 2018. When you think about the relationship between these two numbers, 0.00000978% is a very, very small number.

When I read this information about Tiger Sharks, I was overcome with gratitude and emotion that the shark who bit Juliun did not attack a second time. In a recent article titled, "Tiger Sharks" by National Geographic, the statistics become even more frightening: "These large, blunt-nosed predators have a duly earned reputation as man-eaters. They are second only to great whites in attacking people. But because they have a near completely undiscerning palate, they are not likely to swim away after biting a human, as great whites frequently do" ("Tiger Sharks").

The shark that attacked Juliun likely weighed around 1,000 pounds. The strength and power of a creature this big is hard to comprehend. Juliun and I both love the ocean. We don't want to fear, but it's difficult to come to terms with the attack. We know that "Tiger sharks are common in tropical and sub-tropical waters throughout the world. Large specimens can grow to as much as 20 to 25 feet in length and weigh more than 1,900 pounds" ("Tiger Sharks").

The mouth is one of the scariest aspects of a shark. Inside their huge jaw is something that is equally frightening, their teeth. Molly Edmonds writes that "Each tooth is almost like having several teeth in one space; the sharp, primary cusp extends down, ready to tear into prey. Along the primary cusp, or point, are tiny little serrated cusplets that can saw into the food. The tiger shark has identical upper and lower jaws, and with all these serrated teeth, there's really nothing that the tiger shark can't eat." It's easy to see why sharks do so much damage to their prey.

Chapter 3: A Little History About Us

My happiest childhood memories are of our family vacations to Hawai'i. Frequently, my parents, brothers, sister, and I traveled to Hawai'i for vacations when we were living in both Southern California and Washington State. As a child, I loved playing in the water and building sand boats on the beach with my family. I don't remember thinking about sharks when I was little, but I do remember this changed when I saw *Jaws*, *Jaws 2*, *Jaws 3-D*, and *Jaws: The Revenge*. These movies put fear in me, and as a mom, I am terrified of sharks. I am a mom who knows how to worry, and as you can imagine, I have had a lot to worry about since September 8th.

Juliun was born and raised in Hawai'i. His first trip to the beach took place when he was only a few days old; on this beach outing, he placed his toes in the sand and the water for the first time. Juliun grew up in the ocean and has always loved the water. He started bodyboarding when he was in elementary school. I remember taking him to Kalama Beach, where he spent numerous joyful hours in the beautiful ocean. I would stand and sit on the beach and watch him enjoy each wave. When it was time to go, I would motion for him to come to shore, and he would smile. Juliun would then hold up his pointer finger, signaling to me that he wanted to catch one more wave. One more wave for Juliun usually meant several more waves. As I reflect on these early days, I guess it was inevitable that he would one day take up surfing.

If I were to describe Juliun in a few words, this is what I would say, Juliun is a people person who loves helping and being around others. Juliun is happiest when he is interacting with family, friends, and people he has just met. Juliun refers to everyone he knows as his friend. He is strong, calm, grateful, and extremely cheerful. Juliun is very good at balancing life's stresses, and he truly knows how to enjoy life. Juliun loves basketball, surfing, and most importantly, he loves God.

In the beginning months of 2018, Juliun started surfing. I think he was hooked even before he had his first true ride (catching a wave and standing up on the board for more than a few seconds). From what he's said, this is an incredible feeling, a feeling that only surfers can truly appreciate.

Chapter 4: The Attack

The surfing conditions for September 8th were forecasted to be extraordinary. Hurricane Olivia was heading towards Hawai'i, bringing with it an ocean swell (a.k.a. surfer's delight). These ideal surfing conditions motivated so many to surf near Pounder's on this Saturday morning.

It's important to note that Juliun, like all surfers, is always mindful of sharks. Surfers have a lot to focus on when they are in the ocean, and being on the look-out for sharks is definitely at the forefront of their minds.

Juliun and four friends entered the water around 6:30 a.m.; they were excited, as I'm sure all the surfers were who surfed this spot on September 8th. The winds were light, the waves were big, and it was hard to see because the glare of the sun on the ocean was unusually bright.

When they completed the half-mile paddle to their surfing destination, there were a few other surfers already there. The men who would be Juliun's heroes had not yet entered the water and made the long trek out to the waves. It is truly a blessing that the shark did not attack Juliun earlier, as the men he needed to save his life were not nearby at this time.

At approximately 8:30 a.m., Juliun sat on his eight-foot surfboard, his legs in the water, his arms and hands on his board. He faced the vast ocean, watching some of the surfers surfing this typically deserted spot, when out of the water came the shark. Juliun did not see or hear the shark before it came out of the water and took hold of his right arm. The large creature seemed to go undetected because none of the 30 or so surfers saw it before it jumped out of the water and onto Juliun's arm. Later, someone did say they saw the shark's tail flapping around when the attack happened.

Juliun remembers looking at the shark on his arm and staring briefly into its piercing eyes as he questioned if this was really happening. After several seconds of unimaginable horror, the shark let go, and Juliun's survival instincts kicked in. Wanting the nearby surfers to see what had just happened, Juliun held up his injured arm and started yelling, "Shark, help!" He remembers seeing most of the nearby surfers fleeing to safety towards shore as the blood gushed out of his arm and wrist.

Moments later, a huge wave hit Juliun and thrust him underwater; this powerful wave stripped his surf leash right off his leg, causing him to lose his board. It was at this moment that he thought his life was over. Juliun knew that he had been bitten by a shark, he knew that he was bleeding profusely, he knew that the shark was nearby, he knew that his fellow surfers were swimming to safety, he knew he couldn't paddle/swim the 20+ minutes to shore with one arm and no surfboard, and he knew he was getting pounded by the huge surf.

During these terrifying moments beneath the surface of the water, Juliun said a prayer while the unrelentless ocean tossed him. He prayed for help and then he prayed for his family. He thought his time on earth was finished.

When Juliun resurfaced, he gasped for air. As he looked around, he saw no one. He started swimming towards shore with his uninjured arm while his right arm squirted blood. Juliun could see everything inside his opened arm, right down to the bones. Within a miraculously short period of time, Juliun's heroes started arriving one after another. The miracles that followed, in addition to the miracles that had already taken place, were humbling.

Juliun's absolute fear turned to complete joy when Flynn, Jesse, Bret, Jose, Drew, and Ryan came to the rescue. [1] These earthly angels, whom Juliun had never met before, seemed to have come from out of nowhere, each arriving within seconds of the other. Jesse even had Juliun's surfboard thanks to Mitchell, who retrieved it and handed it off to Jesse before rushing to shore to call 911. It was at this moment that Juliun knew he was going to be okay.

---

[1] We did not include last names for privacy purposes. The names of the heroes are not listed in any particular order. Additionally, we alternate the order of their names at times to emphasize all of their status as heroes.

Chapter 5: Flynn's Account

We are so grateful to share this firsthand account from an exceptional hero who played a crucial part in Juliun's rescue. Flynn shared his story with Juliun one week after the attack, and he gave us permission to include it in our book. As you will see, Flynn is a great man and a gifted writer. Thank you, Flynn!

The morning of Saturday, September 8th is a day I will never forget. It took me about a week to internalize, digest, and formulate understandings of what had happened.

My friend Bret and I were talking Friday night, trying to figure out where we should surf during the upcoming hurricane Olivia swell that was forecasted to arrive overnight with light winds and a good-sized swell. I kinda left the decision up to Bret, and he said, "Let's just go straight to Pounders for first light and take it from there." Something was telling him that would be the place to be for the morning surf session.

The next day, I woke up at my usual 4:30 a.m., coffee, breakfast, feed the dogs, and out the door, driving east. I picked Bret up at his house shortly after and pulled into the Pounders parking lot on the east side by about 7:30 a.m. The surf break is about a half-mile out to sea, and I didn't know what we were looking for while we stood on the beach, squinting out into the bright eastside sunrise glare. Somehow Bret could tell the waves were good out there, and he made the call to paddle out. After applying sunscreen and waxing our boards, we began to walk down the beach, when a friend of mine, Jesse, quickly said good morning as he ran past us. Turns out Jesse had finished his morning husband-and-father duties, and he only had enough time to catch a wave or two before he had to report to work. Bret and I thought his urgency was because of seeing the waves firing a half-mile out to sea, so we decided to run down the beach with him as well.

As we reached the point where you paddle out from, there was a friendly man who quickly introduced himself, and said he had never surfed out at this particular spot before. After we introduced ourselves, he was excited to recognize my name from some surf magazines. I quickly deflected the praises and said that Jesse was "the guy" he needed to know. After we shared some laughs while putting on our leashes while meeting a new friend, we all began the half-mile paddle out to the surf break.

About a third of the way out, we saw our friend Tamayo on his way in already. He had to be at work soon but said that the waves were really good out there. Tamayo's words encouraged us; we felt our long, glared-out paddle wasn't for nothing.

When I finally got out into the lineup, I saw that there were a lot of people surfing out there already! My immediate guess was that there were about 25-30 surfers out. By far, the most people I've seen out at any rare and low-key east side surf spot. The wave itself breaks along a curved-reef drop-off, and can perfectly peel through three defined peaks before it drops off into a deep channel. Because of the thick crowd factor, I decided to stay between the middle and end peak, instead of contesting for waves at the first peak where most of the crowd was posted.

There were a few wide-swinging sets that connected to the middle and end peak, quickly confirming my decision to attempt catching waves towards the end of the reef, instead of sitting with most of the crowd.

We were out for about 15 minutes, and I was paddling back out after my second wave, when I noticed something strange. There was a three-wave set, and about 6-8 people rode on the first two waves. It was strange to see, and I couldn't understand why such a large number of people decided to ride those first two waves together. Another 6-8 people rode on the third wave, and I also saw other people paddling in towards shore. I could tell something was up, and as the third wave peeled past me, a bodyboarder riding in front of the other surfers frantically screamed, "Shark, shark, SHAAAARRRRK!" as they rode the wave past me.

I just thought someone had a shiny watch on, and maybe a large barracuda bit them. As I paddled over the third wave of the set, instead of seeing 30 surfers, there was just one lone ranger out there, sitting on his soft-top longboard looking at his wrist. I was about 50 yards away from him, but I could tell his wrist and arm looked kinda like a noodle, not really working or being held like a normal limb. I continued paddling closer towards this lone ranger, when the wave of the morning showed up, sucking below sea level on the ledge of the reef before pitching a big barrel, top to bottom, directly onto the injured surfer and his board. At this point, I was close enough that when he surfaced after the pounding from that wave, I realized just how injured he was. The turbulent white-water left from the wave that had broke quickly turned dark red around his immediate

13

circumference. He also had lost his board, and he was visibly having trouble staying above the surface with only one arm working.

I do not clearly remember all the details that immediately followed. All I remember is that this guy was hurt and needed help, and a sort of tunnel-vision came over me. I quickly paddled up to him so that he could hang onto my board, and I told him to relax and that he was going to be okay, and that we should start heading in. He settled his breathing and remained as calm as I instructed.

It was then that I realized the extent of his injury; it was most definitely not just a Barracuda bite! From the bottom of his shoulder diagonally to his elbow, ran a shredded wound that was squirting blood, to the beat of his thumping heart. His wrist was also severely gashed, barely connecting his hand by a few tendons. My main concern was to keep him calm, assuring him that he'd be okay, while I took off the Velcro that connected my leash to my board. I knew he needed a tourniquet, but I was unsure how I could effectively tie it around his arm and get him in to shore on my own. I knew that if he continued to lose blood, he would go into shock, and that would be really bad, especially a half-mile out to sea. My second concern was that we were chumming in his blood, there was a large predator swimming below the surface in the immediate area, and I was 100 percent sure it was going to return to its prey.

This day, the large aquatic predator's prey turned out to be Juliun, a 23-year-old Hawai'i resident who had just graduated from BYU Hawai'i. Juliun is a big dude, but obviously does not taste like a fish or sea turtle, and what was presumed to be about a 10-foot Tiger Shark, thankfully, decided that it would go elsewhere after the initial attack.

Luckily, about a minute or two after the wave had taken Juliun's board to the inside of the surf, Jesse came across one of Juliun's friends attempting to paddle the detached soft-top longboard back out but was having trouble. Jesse told the friend to go in and call 911, took the soft-top, and quickly paddled it out to us. It was such a relief to see my friend Jesse paddling back out with a much more buoyant and effective rescue board! At that moment, I remembered the five other surfers, including Bret, who had not completely fled the lineup. They were there to help us get Juliun up and positioned laying on his soft-top.

I threw my surf leash over Juliun to Jesse, "Here, Jesse, tie the tourniquet." He was on Juliun's right side, closest to the wound, and I knew he had medical training. Once the tourniquet was tight above Juliun's wounds, we all took turns pushing Juliun towards shore. We instructed him to stay calm, lay still, and let us do all the work. We had a long way to go, and I noticed his face looked pale and he was still bleeding a lot. About two thirds of the way in, as soon as I was able to touch the bottom with my feet, I ditched my board and slid my hand into Juliun's armpit, and clamped the artery that I could feel pumping. I kept pressure there with my hand, and I never let go until we loaded him into the ambulance about 30 minutes later.

Getting Juliun out of danger was nothing short of a group effort, and it helped me to know that I had friends there who I could trust. I knew they weren't going to panic or run away, so I'm sure that helped Juliun as well!

When I look at the whole situation and the decisions that were made ahead of time to get us all there at that same moment, I know there was some divine intervention or something else that helped a nightmarish situation turn into a smooth, effective, and successful rescue. I believe everything happens for a reason; we are all part of a bigger picture. At the very least, we can look at this experience as a sign; we were all in the place that we were meant to be at that moment.

Chapter 6: The Miraculous Rescue

We have all heard the word "hero" before, and I'm sure this word means different things to different people. To me, the word "hero" has a whole new meaning now. Hero is a word that I use reverently, humbly, and emotionally. The heroes that went to Juliun's rescue were completely selfless. They knew there was a large predator looming below, they knew there was a lot of blood in the water, they knew it was a long way to shore, and they knew that everyone else had fled to safety. Jesse, Bret, Jose, Drew, Ryan, and Flynn are true heroes who completely focused on helping a young man in dire need.

Juliun, lying on his stomach on the board, remembers being surrounded by these men who would save his life. Jesse and Flynn applied two tourniquets to Juliun's bicep; they used surf leashes for tourniquets. This life-saving task would have been even more difficult, if not impossible, if the ocean had not calmed, but it miraculously did. After they applied the tourniquets, they pushed Juliun on his board, and the half-mile paddle to safety began.

The six men took turns pushing and paddling while Juliun lay on his board, trying to paddle with his left arm. "Thank you," he said. "Thank you." He said it over and over and over again to his new friends. Concerned that Juliun's energy level was dropping, they simultaneously told Juliun to lay still, be quiet, and let them do the work.

During this miraculous rescue, Juliun continued losing blood despite the two tourniquets. More needed to be done to prevent continuous blood loss. Thinking quickly,

Flynn clamped and held Juliun's axillary artery, stopping the flow enough to aid in this dire situation.

The heroes paddled straight ahead, pushing Juliun's board. They made it to shore in about seven minutes. The family who owns the house near the shore where they landed had just put up a retaining wall and staircase; the men used this staircase to transport Juliun from the ocean to the top of the driveway where they would meet the ambulance. While waiting for the ambulance, Juliun remembers receiving an abundance of love and support from everyone present.

Chapter 7: The Ambulance Arrives

When the ambulance arrived, Flynn, who was still clamping Juliun's axillary artery, assisted the paramedics in placing Juliun into the ambulance. Korey and Kylan, brilliant paramedics who came to transport Juliun to Queen's (Oahu's trauma hospital), stepped into action. The distance from Pounder's to Queen's is 32 miles, and when the roads are clear, the driving time is one hour. Korey and Kylan, who typically service other parts of the island, just happened to be substituting for the regular paramedics who service this area.

As the ambulance departed the scene, lights flashing and sirens blaring, Korey replaced the two surf leash tourniquets with a formal CAT medical tourniquet while Kylan drove as fast as he could. Korey started an IV and stabilized Juliun the best he could. They arrived at the hospital at 9:34 a.m.

Upon entering the hospital, they were met by the fully activated trauma team, and the team rushed Juliun into surgery. Juliun was in hemorrhagic shock, which means that his body was starting to shut down due to blood loss. Juliun's blood pressure was dangerously low, and his heart rate was abnormally rapid.

The doctors gave Juliun anesthesia, and he remembers asking the doctors if they could save his arm. "We may have to amputate part of it," a doctor said. These are the last words Juliun heard before going into unconsciousness.

Juliun had two large openings in his arm, one by his elbow and the other on his wrist. The laceration by his elbow measured 17 cm long, 5 cm wide, and 4 cm deep. Juliun also had three deep puncture wounds on the bottom of his arm; the shark's top and bottom teeth both reached Juliun's bones.

Chapter 8: Surgery

When I arrived at the emergency room, Juliun had already gone into surgery. I told the front desk who I was, and they escorted me to a small, windowless room with a few chairs. I sat waiting in this tiny room, and I prayed. I didn't know anything but that a shark had bitten my son. I tried to share my fear, concern, and worry with God, but I'm a worrier. I prayed. I waited.

After a few minutes alone, a hospital social worker entered. She told me Juliun was in surgery, and then she went to get one of the doctors to come and talk to me. When the doctor entered the room, I noticed how worried he looked. He said that Juliun had lost a lot of blood and would probably need a transfusion. I asked if I could give my blood, but he said that would take too long. Our conversation was very short, and I don't remember what else was said. What I do recall vividly was the concern I saw on his face.

After the doctor left, the social worker asked me a few questions before escorting me to the surgery waiting room. She told me she would come and get me when Juliun was out of surgery.

I tried my best to sit, think positive thoughts, have faith, and be calm. I took many deep breaths. There was one other person in the waiting room: another mom waiting for her son. After sitting in silence for what felt like a long, long time, we started talking. She told me her son had been in a moped accident and had severe injuries to his leg and face.

She shared that she had seen him before he went into surgery. To me, this mom seemed remarkably calm; I knew she was struggling, but she was holding it together.

"I'm waiting for my son," I said. I told her he was in surgery. She asked me what happened. "Shark. He was bitten by a shark," I said. I couldn't believe what I had just said. *My son has been bitten by a shark, and now he is fighting for his life.* I am sitting in a hospital waiting room, and all I can do is pray for him right now. I can't do anything else but pray and try to stay calm. Nothing seemed to make sense.

I believe in prayer and I know the power of prayer. I have heard of miracles before, and I have seen miracles happen to people I love. Miracles come from God, and I have great faith in Him. With all this knowledge, I was now being given the hardest test of my life. I needed to be strong, calm, and grateful for the things that I knew to be true. I needed to hold tight to the faith I had in His power. And I needed to believe that everything was going to be okay.

The skilled trauma team of doctors and nurses worked on Juliun for nearly three hours. They stopped the bleeding, got Juliun's vital signs under control, explored the injuries to his right arm, cleaned the wounds extensively, and ordered several tests to better understand the extent of his injuries. They left Juliun's wounds open for two reasons: additional surgery the following day and concern for infection. I believe they were more worried about infection from the ocean water than they were from the shark's mouth.

Chapter 9: Intensive Care Unit

It was about 1 p.m. when the social worker came to get me. I followed her into the elevator and down long hallways until we arrived in the Surgical Trauma Intensive Care Unit (ICU) room 459. I was grateful that Juliun was out of surgery, and elated that I was about to see him.

When we entered the room, he was sitting up, and as he looked at me, he smiled. My son was alive! And, my son had his arm! I quickly walked to the side of his bed and kissed him. I was so grateful, so happy, and so relieved. God had blessed Juliun with an abundance of miracles, and He had answered my prayers. This was truly an incredible moment that I will never forget.

I stood there hugging my son. "Are you okay?" I asked him.

Juliun's first words to me were, "Mom, I'm okay." These are the same three words he had said to me when he was in the ambulance. Juliun was okay. Juliun was better than okay. Juliun was filled with joy for the miracles he had received.

Juliun said that when he had first woken up from surgery, he looked at his arm to see if it was still there. His arm was completely wrapped up, and all we could see were his fingertips. His fingers felt a little cool, and they looked slightly pale. He had minimal sensation when I touched his fingers.

Medical staff (doctors, nurses, technicians) monitored Juliun closely. Every hour, he was given a Doppler Ultrasound to measure the amount of blood flow through his arteries and veins near his wrist; the medical staff were concerned about a possible lack of adequate circulation to his arm, wrist, and fingers.

The main injuries Juliun suffered from the shark bite were:

- Right arm radial nerve laceration with no motor function to his wrist or hand.

- Right wrist multiple extensor tendon lacerations.

- Right forearm radial sensory nerve laceration.

There are five major nerves in the arm, and three of these five innervate the sensory and motor components of the hand. The radial nerve is responsible for wrist and finger extension, partial sensation to the hand and forearm, and it innervates muscles on the back of the arm. The shark severed Juliun's radial nerve by his elbow at the place where the nerve branches.

I hadn't been with Juliun too long before a hospital staff member came and took him for tests. I remember walking the hallways and seeing patients in need, some in great need. Some people had loved ones at their bedside and others were alone. I felt tremendous compassion for the people I saw. Hospitals are happy places for some and sad places for others.

When the nurse wheeled Juliun back into his room, he was happy because he had made a new friend (the technician who performed his scan). As I mentioned earlier, Juliun is happiest when he is interacting with people. He is so good at making connections with people and helping them to feel comfortable. I am blessed with a wonderful son!

While human interaction plays a significant role in Juliun's happiness, food comes second. I think most young men feel this way. Shortly after returning from his scan, his nurse brought in a tray of hospital food. This meal was Juliun's first since the attack, and he was exceptionally hungry.

Juliun is right-handed, and it was difficult for him to eat with his left hand. This task was the beginning of learning how to be ambidextrous. Trying to feed himself when he was ravenously hungry was probably an ideal time to learn how to use his other hand because he was highly motivated. Juliun didn't eat as much as I thought he would. The unimaginable events of the day, exhaustion, shock, pain, and concern for the upcoming surgery started to take a toll. On the outside, Juliun seemed strong, calm, and grateful, and I believe he was the same way on the inside despite the events. These overwhelming feelings started to get the better of me, too.

Juliun did not sleep well the first night. As you can imagine, there were many reasons for his restlessness—the noisy machines attached to him, the hourly Doppler test, oral and intravenous medication, the hospital staff checking on him, pain, the position and weight of the bandages on his arm, and the unknown. Even more significant reasons for sleeplessness: the thoughts and dreams he had about the shark he saw on his arm, and the leg compression pump that inflated the leg wraps on his legs. Every time the compression leg wraps inflated, Juliun thought the shark was biting his legs. Every time

he closed his eyes, he saw the shark on his arm.

Chapter 10: Surgery Number Two

A team of doctors and residents arrived early Sunday morning to examine Juliun and talk about the surgery plans for the day. Queen's Hospital is a teaching hospital, so there are many physicians in training. The doctors and residents gathered in a circle around a large computer on wheels and talked about each patient before entering their room. After the examinations took place, they exited the patient room and again gathered together to further discuss the findings of the checkups. Because shark attacks are so rare, Juliun's case fascinated all the medical staff, especially the residents.

Juliun's surgery schedule changed a couple times throughout the night and morning. His late afternoon surgery, scheduled for Sunday afternoon, meant that Juliun was allowed to eat an early breakfast. By this time, he was famished and parched. He ate everything on his plate and would have loved to have had a second helping of each item. Surgery requires fasting, and he knew he wouldn't have more food for 12 hours. Unfortunately, this was not the time for seconds. It was a little before 7 a.m. when he finished his breakfast, and the nurses allowed him to drink small amounts of water and have ice chips until 9 a.m. It wasn't long after the nurses took the ice chips that Juliun's mouth became dry, and he wanted more water. I don't know if his thirst was the result of salt in his breakfast or his medications. Either way, it was hard to see him so thirsty and even harder to not give him water to drink.

Several friends had come to the hospital to visit on Saturday and Sunday. News of the attack had already hit social media and was now making its way to local and national news. Family, friends, and strangers around the world were praying for Juliun (and me). The prayers gave us strength, comfort, and peace.

The anesthesiologist, assigned to Juliun's surgery, came to see us early Sunday afternoon. He asked several questions about Juliun's medical history and shared important information with us. The doctor was attentive, conscientious, and personable. He was also very kind and patient, especially with our questions.

Shortly after the anesthesiologist left, the orthopedic surgeon on call who would be performing Juliun's surgery arrived. He examined Juliun, asked questions, shared information, and answered our questions. This double board-certified Orthopedic and Hand Surgeon was compassionate, experienced, and ready for surgery.

The operating room became available earlier than expected, and the doctors were eager to start. Juliun, on the other hand, was not ready because of the food he ate for breakfast. For safety reasons, all food intake is supposed to stop eight hours before surgery.

Sharks and surgery were two things that frightened Juliun; two things he never wanted to encounter or experience. In a matter of 30 short hours, he had lived through both, and he now waited for a second surgery to begin. I don't know what his thoughts and feelings were at this time, but I do know that this remarkable young man was definitely being blessed and strengthened.

When the time came to wheel Juliun to the operating room, I walked alongside his bed. I wanted to be by his side every second I could. If they would have let me, I would have walked right into the operating room with him. At the entrance to the operating rooms, I asked the doctor to treat Juliun like he would his own son. The doctor smiled and said, "I try to always remember this." I kissed Juliun, told him I loved him, and I watched his bed roll away and the doors close in front of me.

I tried to stay composed as I quickly walked to the nearest bathroom. As soon as I closed and locked the door, I crumbled to the floor in tears. The worry and stress of the previous 30+ hours took over, and in the privacy of this small hospital bathroom, I melted down and released my emotions. I wept and prayed, wept and prayed, and wept and prayed. I then cleaned my face, took some deep breaths, and hurried to the waiting room.

The waiting room was quiet and empty. I sat, paced, took deep breaths, and prayed constantly, for nearly four hours. At one point I did pick up the hospital phone to ask how things were going. I don't remember exactly what was said, but I do remember being told it was still going to be a while longer.

When the surgeon entered the waiting room, I hugged him. I listened as carefully as I could and tried my best to take notes. I asked many questions and needed him to repeat things several times. He was extremely patient and kind. He told me what he did, and then he shared what needed to be done next month. The doctor had repaired three big muscles by Juliun's elbow and four tendons at his wrist. The bite went to Juliun's joints but did not damage them. The joints and other injuries were explored and thoroughly irrigated. The shark cut Juliun's radial nerve at his elbow; this is the spot where the nerve divides into deep and superficial branches (motor and sensory).

The surgeon tagged these nerve ends so that they could be found and repaired at Juliun's next surgery. The doctor then closed all five wounds— three small wounds on the back of his arm, and the two large wounds at his elbow and wrist. The team then bandaged Juliun's arm--splinted it at his elbow, wrist and thumb, and then bandaged it again. The doctor said that Juliun was in recovery, and I would be able to see him soon. Filled with appreciation and gratitude, I thanked the doctor repeatedly and watched him walk down the hall.

Within seconds, I bowed my head and expressed my deepest thanksgiving to God for the glorious miracles Juliun had received. Juliun survived a shark attack, brilliant heroes came to his rescue, the skilled paramedics got him to the hospital in time, the talented emergency room full trauma team was in place and ready to do all that was needed to save Juliun's life and his arm, and the gifted orthopedic surgeon had just repaired Juliun's lacerated muscles and tendons. God was near, and miracles happen.

The surgeon walked passed the waiting room about 15 minutes later and seemed surprised that I was still there. He escorted me through a locked door and down a hallway to the recovery room. He knew how much I wanted to see Juliun, and he didn't want me to have to wait any longer. I thanked him for this and quickly walked to Juliun's bed. Juliun was lying down, and a nurse was by his side. He seemed semi-alert and looked remarkably well for what he had just been through. I took his left hand in mine. We were both so grateful that the surgery was over.

A second nurse came a short time later, and together they pushed Juliun's bed back to his ICU room. They told Juliun that he could eat, and even though he didn't feel too hungry, he was happy to hear these words. After resting for a little while, I asked if he could get up and stretch his legs. Juliun had not walked for 36 hours, and I felt it was important for him to get out of bed and move around. My request surprised the nurse, and before she said yes, she needed to check with the doctor on duty. The nurse said that people in ICU do not normally ask to get up and walk.

Going for a little walk was not an easy task. Juliun needed to be unplugged from the machines, his IV needed to be transferred to a pole with wheels, he needed to put a second gown on to cover his back, and he needed slippers on his feet. For a young man as healthy and active as Juliun, this was a new experience. When he finally got to his feet, the weight and bulk of his splints shocked him. His right arm, which was splinted at a 90-degree angle, needed considerable support. The nurse pushed Juliun's IV pole on the left side, Juliun carried his right arm with his left hand, and I held onto Juliun's right side for support. We walked two short laps around the ICU, and then Juliun got back in bed. Even though this was an unusual stroll, Juliun was touched by the other patients he saw lying in their ICU beds; his injured arm did not seem quite so challenging when he saw what others were going through.

Our second night was rougher than our first night. Juliun started bleeding through his bandages, and his blood pressure spiked. He also felt like he was losing even more feeling in his fingers. The resident, who assisted the orthopedic surgeon, was still on duty, and she came to examine Juliun. Throughout all the events over the last two days, Juliun remained strong, calm, and grateful. I, on the other hand, did not feel very strong or calm. I was very grateful though. On this stressful night, all I could do was one of the three.

When morning arrived, a team of doctors and residents greeted Juliun. They gathered in the hallway, as they had previously, and then entered the room in full force. The doctors asked several questions, examined Juliun, and then said that Juliun was stable enough to be discharged that afternoon. I had mixed emotions. I was both happy and scared. I was happy that he was stable and scared about the responsibility of caring for such a large wound. Being surrounded by medical experts gave us a feeling of safety and assurance that help was nearby if needed. Nevertheless, it was time to go home and start the healing process.

Chapter 11: Healing at Home

It was late afternoon on Monday, September 10th, when we left the hospital. Juliun had a temporary splint on his elbow, arm, wrist, and hand that was very bulky and heavy. The medical staff gave us instructions, papers, and lots of medications, right before the wheelchair arrived. The nurse pushed Juliun down the long hospital hallways and out the main entrance doors where I met him with the car. Juliun was happy to see the sun, breathe fresh air, and be on his way home; he left the hospital with a smile.

When we arrived home, things felt a little different. Things were different. Juliun's phone exploded with messages from family, friends, and people he didn't know. Everyone wanted to see him and hear about what happened. We weren't home long before people started coming over. Ryan, one of the heroes who saved Juliun's life, was one of the first people to stop by. This was a special visit. I had never met Ryan, and when he walked through the door, I felt like he was one of my best friends, a friend that I would be forever grateful for.

We took pictures of everyone who came to visit; this was Juliun's idea. We also took pictures of people we went to visit. In each photo, Juliun is smiling, always smiling. These pictures not only tell a miraculous story, but they also tell about the importance of recognizing/acknowledging blessings and expressing gratitude as soon as possible. Juliun and I had thanked the doctors, nurses, and hospital staff. We also thanked family and friends for their love and prayers. And, we had thanked Ryan. It was now time to thank the other five men who so heroically safeguarded Juliun's life.

Early Tuesday morning, we drove to Pupukea, on Oahu's North Shore, to thank Bret, Jose, Drew, Flynn, and Jesse. Juliun and I hugged each brave man and expressed our heartfelt appreciation. These amazing men were just as happy to see Juliun as he was to see them. They gathered close together and talked about the incredible events that took place three days prior. Jose, Drew, Ryan, Flynn, Bret, Jesse, and Juliun all saw God's hand in this experience. The heroes knew there was divine intervention, and they knew they were all surfing this precise spot on this exact day and time for a reason.

After our supercalifragilisticexpialidocious visit with Drew, Flynn, Jesse, Bret, and Jose, we left Pupukea and drove south towards Pounders. We made two stops along the way to thank additional people who helped after the attack; Juliun had a strong need to thank everyone who helped him.

Our final stop for the morning was the house near Pounders where the ambulance arrived. This was the home of Tiffany and Noah, both of whom were at home. Juliun had never met Tiffany before the attack— just like he had never met Ryan, Jesse, Bret, Jose, Flynn, or Drew prior to the shark bite. (Noah was not home when the incident happened, so Juliun and I were both meeting him for the first time this morning.) Tiffany shared with us what she saw both in the ocean and in her driveway on September 8th.

That morning, Tiffany looked out her window, thinking she had never seen so many surfers surfing this spot. When Juliun was brought out of the water and helped up to Tiffany's carport to wait for the ambulance, she gave him towels to help with the bleeding, and she watched him closely for symptoms of shock.

Tiffany and Noah were happy that Juliun was alive, and that he had his arm. We walked across their yard to the shoreline and looked at the spot where the attack happened. Noah said that they had just constructed a rock staircase in their retaining wall for easy access to the ocean. This new, operational staircase was one of the numerous blessings Juliun received three days prior. Noah also said that there were tourists vacationing in the house next to the staircase, and that these people were praying for Juliun.

Tuesday afternoon, Juliun had an appointment with his primary care doctor, who is a special friend that we have known for many years. This accomplished physician, who just happens to know quite a bit about sharks, spent time listening, answering our questions, reading the hospital notes, and talking about Juliun's injuries. He looked at Juliun's fingers and checked his circulation; the bandages had not been removed but were going to be removed the next day when Juliun went to see the occupational therapist (OT). He said that the bite just missed Juliun's radial artery; this was another miracle from God.

On Wednesday morning, we went to see the OT to pick up a more comfortable, usable splint. The therapists who specialized in hand rehabilitation were so skilled and kind. They removed Juliun's bandages, and we saw his arm for the first time since the trauma. As the two therapists gently unwrapped the multiple layers of bandages, I felt apprehensive. I wanted to be strong and put on a brave face for Juliun. To my surprise, Juliun's arm looked much better than I'd anticipated. There were two large lacerations with lots of stitches; one near his elbow running down the inside of his forearm and the other one on top of his wrist. The skin on the top, middle part, of his forearm was unblemished. There were also a few small cuts on the bottom of his forearm that had a bundle of stitches close together. The part that was the hardest for me to bear was the limpness of Juliun's arm; it was as if he had no functioning muscles to lift or move his elbow, lower arm, and hand.

The therapists talked about wound care, told us things to look for, and fitted Juliun for a breathable, durable, plastic elbow, and forearm splint. The forearm splint, which supported his thumb, palm, wrist, and forearm, was attached first and then the elbow splint overlapped the lower splint and extended several inches above Juliun's elbow. These two black splints were substantial, yet relatively lightweight, especially compared to the plaster (cement) blocks that had just been removed.

Our first few days home were busy, and Juliun seemed to be sleeping reasonably well; this was a blessing, and we were grateful. I, on the other hand, slept with one eye and both ears open. I think mothers have an instinctive monitoring system, like the hospital vital machines. Even though Juliun was not hooked up to a machine anymore, my internal monitoring system was working overtime. I was worrying about the past, present, and future. There were times when my emotions became too much to bear, and I started crying. There were also times when I thought about all the things that happened and God's miracles were so clear, that I started crying because I was so grateful. I prefer the grateful tears!

During the next couple of weeks, I did my best to take care of Juliun's physical wounds. The first time I unwrapped his arm to clean it and put new pads and bandages on, I took pictures so I could replace everything the way it was before I started. I made frequent trips to the drug store to buy supplies, and I remember thinking our small home was beginning to look like a mini emergency room and pharmacy.

Television and newspaper reporters, along with local and national shark experts, contacted Juliun to learn more about his shark attack. Mitchell, Juliun's friend who retrieved his surfboard and called 911, started a Go Fund Me page, which initiated some of the above phone calls. Juliun was always happy to talk about his encounter with anyone who had questions. Juliun was even more delighted to express his gratitude to God, the heroes, paramedics, doctors, nurses, therapists, and everyone else who had helped.

Chapter 12: Preparing for the Next Shark Bite

Juliun had his first follow-up appointment with the orthopedic surgeon on Monday, September 24th. This doctor, who repaired Juliun's muscles and tendons fifteen days before, had been away at a medical conference back east for the past two weeks. The doctor, Juliun, and I were all happy to be reunited. We had many questions to ask the doctor, and we were very grateful for the time he spent answering them.

The doctor removed Juliun's stitches at this visit, and his lacerations looked remarkably healed. The doctor and nurse placed Steristrips and a special adhesive along the length of the wounds to aid with continued skin closure and healing. They instructed us to keep these strips dry and in place for as long as possible.

In addition, we talked about next steps. The original plan was to do a nerve graft in early October (four weeks after the attack). This was still the plan, but instead of four weeks, the doctor now said six weeks. I believe there were several reasons for this time change, one of which was to give Juliun more time to heal between surgeries. I remember the surgeon saying, "When I go in there again, it is going to be like another shark bite." This was extremely difficult to hear. Most of what the doctor said was over our heads, and we struggled to make sense of the injuries, the repairs that had already been done, and the remaining reconstruction.

As the days passed, Juliun and I had some new trials. Juliun began having flashbacks and nightmares, which made deep, restful sleep nearly impossible. Juliun saw the shark attacking him in his dreams, and he would lie awake for hours, staring at his surfboard in the corner of his room. I pleaded with him to move the board to another room, thinking this would help. Juliun insisted that he needed to keep it in his room in order to face his fears. I did my best to understand and be respectful of his need. As much as I wanted to take control of everything that had happened and was happening, I knew I didn't have the power to accomplish this. I wanted to make everything better, and I wanted more than anything to turn back the clock to the morning of September 8th and undo the shark attack.

Throughout the trials we faced, God was near. The heroes, along with family and friends, were also present, giving Juliun constant support. Juliun even received a phone call from Jamie, a famous surfer, who expressed his aloha and well wishes. These loving interactions always gave Juliun a big and needed boost.

Juliun reached out to other shark attack victims to help with his flashbacks and nightmares. These admirable individuals understood the trauma that occurs after being bitten by a shark. I was grateful that Juliun talked to these amazing shark attack survivors, and I was even more grateful that the knowledge they shared was empowering the healing process.

Juliun had regular appointments with the orthopedic surgeon and occupational hand therapist, in the weeks ahead. At every appointment, when the doctor entered or exited the exam room, Juliun stood and extended his left hand in order to shake the doctor's hand. Juliun was starting to make visual progress, and we were excited to share each milestone with the doctor and therapist. The appointments always started happy, but we usually left feeling drained. It took me time to figure out why. The appointments were emotional and mental; I tried so hard to better understand what was happening and what was going to happen. For Juliun, the appointments were emotional, mental, and physical. He, too, was trying to understand the extent of his injuries, ask questions, and do the tasks he was being asked to do. The mental focus we gave at each appointment, along with the emotional and physical components, were some of the reasons why I believe we left these appointments feeling so weary.

I attempted to research nerve injuries and nerve grafts on the internet. Juliun's injury was not common, and, therefore, it was hard to find articles to read. When I did find something, I didn't understand it. When I found a video to watch, I cried. I was grateful to have three local doctor friends who answered my questions.

As the surgery date approached, we became more anxious with each new day. The planned day changed four times (scheduling and illness postponements) before the surgery actually happened; this added to our stress. The orthopedic surgeon wanted the same anesthesiologist who worked with him in the last surgery to assist him with this one. There were two main reasons for this: patients woke up feeling better under the care of this anesthesiologist, and the surgeon wanted a skilled anesthesiologist to assist him with Juliun's intricate and long surgery.

The surgical plan included harvesting the sural nerve from the back of Juliun's right lower leg and grafting this to his right arm. The sural nerve is a sensory nerve that provides sensation/feeling to the heel, ankle, and outside of the foot. The sural nerve is the go-to nerve when a transplant is needed. We, especially me, struggled with this plan because there was so much we didn't understand. I knew Juliun's legs were healthy and strong, but I worried about the risk of this procedure. I didn't want to do anything to hurt his leg temporarily or permanently. Once this nerve was taken and transplanted, there was no changing our mind; we would have to live with this decision forever.

They gave Juliun the option to have a nerve transplant from a donor. However, there would be no details about the person whose nerve it was, and there was no guarantee that Juliun's body would accept it. I wanted to give Juliun my nerve and leave his unharmed leg alone. I couldn't bear the thought of anything causing him any more harm. Juliun did not want to take my nerve. The last option was not to repair the nerve and live with the damage that had happened. Juliun wanted to do everything he could to have the best chance of a full recovery; as worried as I was, I understood his desire and supported him completely.

Chapter 13: November 10, 2018

Surgery day arrived with little sleep the night before. We, especially Juliun, were trying to be strong, calm, and grateful amidst our tremendous concern over what was about to happen. We left home a little after 5 a.m. to be at the surgery center by 6 a.m. When we arrived, we had difficulty getting into the secure building; the elevators were not working and the stairwell was locked. The large building only had a few lights on, and we didn't see any lights on the floor where we were scheduled to be. We wondered if we had the dates wrong. After a short wait and a few phone calls, we got in touch with the receptionist who came down and escorted us into the elevator.

When we entered the reception area, the receptionist gave Juliun papers to fill out. It was clear that there was only a small staff on hand this early Saturday morning; we were so grateful for each of them, and I prayed to God to guide the hands of those who would be helping with the surgery.

Within minutes of turning in the paperwork, the nurse came to get Juliun. She said she would come back and get me after Juliun had been prepped. It was hard to see Juliun walk away. My waiting period began.

The anesthesiologist came and spoke to me. He is such a kind, gentle man who listens with his heart. I shared some history with him, and he told me about the plan. Our talk was brief, and I was grateful for the few minutes I had with him. I know that he is highly skilled and competent.

It seemed liked a long while passed, and I wondered if the nurse forgot to come

and get me. I started feeling like I needed to see Juliun and tell him that I loved him. The

operating rooms were behind locked doors, and the receptionist who helped us check-in

had gone home. I said a prayer, paced the waiting room floor, and waited as patiently as I

could.

When the locked door opened and the nurse walked towards me, I was so happy.

Surgery had not even started and I was already a mess. I took a deep breath, put on my

brave face, and walked through the door to Juliun. He was sitting up in bed. He smiled,

and I smiled back at him. My son was about to undergo an unimaginable surgery, and I

would have done anything to trade places with him. I tried to be as strong as I could

while in his presence; he was doing that for me, and I needed to do the same for him.

The orthopedic surgeon entered the room with a smile, and we asked him how he

was. The doctor had been sick a few days earlier, and we were praying that he was fully

healed and ready to repair Juliun's injuries with precision and perfection. I know the

surgeon cared deeply for Juliun. I also know that he knew how much I loved my son and

that this was extremely hard for both of us. He said that the surgery would take around

eight hours; he encouraged me to go home or at least go downstairs and get something to

eat. I appreciated his concern, but there was no way I was going to leave this office. I was

going to stay as close as I possibly could.

I pleaded with the doctors and assistants to take good care of Juliun. The

anesthesiologist gave Juliun some medication. I stood by my son's side until they wheeled him through the doorway into the operating room. After, I walked out the locked door and into the waiting room. The time was 7:38 a.m., and my fervent, wholehearted prayers began. I sat and prayed, I stood and prayed, I walked and prayed, and when I was in the privacy of the bathroom, I knelt and prayed.

There was a picture hanging on the waiting room wall of a man surfing with a beautiful rainbow in the background. Years ago, I heard that rainbows are a sign of better days to come; this thought has given me comfort many times throughout my life, and it was something I was going to hold onto that day. As I stood and looked at this picture, I could see Juliun on his board riding the wave with a gigantic smile. Juliun loves the ocean and it has brought him so much joy for the last 20+ years. It was still hard to believe that he had been bitten by a shark exactly nine weeks ago while doing something that gave him so much happiness.

During the next several hours, I read the scriptures, journaled, walked the halls, and prayed. Despite my excessive worrying, I had peace. The peace I felt was comforting and powerful. I know this peace came from a loving Heavenly Father who heard my prayers and the prayers of our family and friends. God was near. I felt His presence, and I knew He was with Juliun. I also knew He was with the doctors, nurses, and others who were assisting in the operating room.

At 3:38 p.m., a staff member told me that the surgery was over. I remember taking a picture of the clock on the wall when I received this long-awaited, much-welcomed news. The orthopedic surgeon's prediction of eight hours was exactly right. I had two questions for the gentleman who was standing in front of me: How was Juliun? When could I see him? This kind man said that the doctors would come out and see me when they were done, and I would be able to see Juliun when he was in the recovery room. I said a prayer and thanked Heavenly Father for *ALL* that He had done for Juliun and me this day.

It was 4:30 p.m. when the orthopedic surgeon came out to speak to me. As I did before, after the last surgery on September 9th, I hugged him and thanked him with emotion and tears. I tried to listen as carefully as I could to the information he shared with me. The surgeon smiled as he said the nerve they took from his right leg was about as perfect as they come. He said that Juliun had a lot, a real lot, of scar tissue in his arm from the trauma and previous two surgeries. Scar tissue is a natural part of healing, and the fact that Juliun had so much meant that he was healthy and he heals well. However, the scar tissue made the surgery more difficult, but the sural nerve was successfully transplanted into Juliun's arm and a tendon transfer in his wrist was completed. The radial nerve ends that had been cut by the shark and tagged at the last surgery, needed to be trimmed back to the point where they were healthy before attaching the sural nerve to the ends. I believe two of the three branched nerve endings were repaired with the sural nerve.

After we finished speaking, I asked the surgeon if I could take a picture of him and the anesthesiologist to share with Juliun later. He replied with a smiley yes and went to get the anesthesiologist. I refer to these two men as the "Dream Team," and I am so grateful for all that they have done for Juliun. I am also extremely grateful for the hard work they put in leading up to this day; they have both spent many, many years preparing themselves to accomplish what they did today.

Within a few minutes of my request for a picture of the Dream Team, I had both doctors in their surgical clothing standing in front of me with a smile. I took their picture and thanked them profusely. They said that the nurse would be out shortly to bring me in to see Juliun. The anesthesiologist said that Juliun did well, despite the long, intricate surgery. He continued, saying that Juliun had eight hours of anesthetics, and it would take time for these drugs to wear off. The anesthesiologist recommended lots of fluids to help flush the medication out of Juliun's system. I expressed my deep gratitude for all he did to care for Juliun and keep him safe. After our conversation ended, the anesthesiologist walked through the locked door, and I stood quietly waiting for my turn.

At 4:50 p.m. the locked door opened, and the nurse came out to get me. It had been a little more than nine hours since I left Juliun's side, and I was eager to see him. When I walked in the room, the first thing I saw was a smile; it was the most beautiful smile I had ever seen. Juliun had just woken up and was lying at a 45-degree angle. As I walked closer, I noticed many things which activated my sense of worry. Juliun had an oxygen tube in his nose, he had wires hooked up to his chest, he had a monitor on his finger, bandages and an IV on his left hand, a blood pressure cuff on his left arm, a pillow on his chest to elevate his right arm, thick massive bandages on his right arm and leg, large ice packs on his right leg, his skin looked pale, one eye was partially closed, and his body looked like he had been through serious trauma. In spite of all this, my precious son was smiling.

I tried my best to be strong, and I hoped the worry I felt did not show on my face. I thought back to when I first saw him after the shark attack, and he had looked so much healthier then. I also remember that the doctor said when he goes back in there to harvest the sural nerve from the back of Juliun's right lower leg and graft this to his right arm, it is going to be like another shark attack. The doctor was right, except that this time it was his arm and leg. As my worry increased, I silently started questioning the decision to have this surgery. I thought, *how in the world could I have let this happen to my son?*

As these thoughts came to mind, I stood next to Juliun's bed and told him that I loved him. I asked him how he was, and he said he felt like he was going to throw up. The nurse said this was normal after surgery. Just then, the two doctors walked in, and she asked them if she could give Juliun some medicine for nausea. The doctors said yes, and the nurse gave Juliun two medications for nausea. The orthopedic surgeon and the anesthesiologist had just stopped by to see Juliun before they left to go home.

Shortly after the doctors left, the nurse had Juliun stand as she wanted him to go to the bathroom. When Juliun transitioned from the 45-degree angle to a sitting position, he felt dizzy. When Juliun tried to stand, with the nurse on one side and me on the other side, he started vomiting and losing his balance. Juliun could not put any weight on his right foot because it was both numb and painful. Every time Juliun moved, he felt like throwing up. The nurse insisted that this was normal, and she wanted him to move anyway. I wanted him to stay put.

When the vomiting stopped, we again tried to have him stand and walk to the bathroom with assistance. After every movement, lying to sitting and sitting to standing, Juliun needed to be still until the dizziness and nausea subsided. Several minutes later, Juliun lifted his right foot to take his first step, and he again started to lose his balance. He said his foot felt like a basketball, and he had no control of it. The nurse got a wheelchair and pushed Juliun into the bathroom that was only a few feet away from the bed.

While the two of them were in the bathroom, I realized that my belief was that Juliun needed to be in the hospital and recover there for a couple days. I did not know how I was going to get him from the car into our house, which included a flight of stairs. I was also concerned about taking care of these two large wounds, his dizziness, repeated vomiting, and flushing his body of all the medication he had been given. I started to panic as I worried about all these things. The doctors had gone home, and I knew the nurse wanted to do the same.

When the nurse came out of the bathroom, I asked her quietly if I could take Juliun to the hospital. I shared my concerns with her, but she said it is best for him to go home. I asked her why he was vomiting when he had been given two anti-vomiting medications, and I wanted to know why he couldn't bear weight on his right foot. The answers I received did not make sense, nor were they comforting. I believe the anti-vomiting medications caused a reaction with all the other medications he had been given, and this was what caused the excessive vomiting. Everything felt overwhelming, and I was not even the person going through this. Instead, I was the mom who would have done anything and everything to help her suffering child, anything.

After spending several minutes in the bathroom, Juliun returned to the bed, where he sat as the nurse and I helped prepare him to go home. Juliun's arm was splinted and bandaged at a 90-degree angle; the weight and bulk of these items made ordinary tasks challenging. Juliun's leg was bandaged almost as thick as his arm, and he had ice packs tied to the bandages. The bulk and weight of these items had the same effect as the bandages on his arm. Juliun's right side needed a lot of help and healing.

At about 6:45 p.m., the nurse felt Juliun was ready to leave. We had been in this surgery center for 12 hours and 45 minutes. The nurse gave us medication, instructions, and paperwork before pushing Juliun's wheelchair to our car. All of the movement and motion added to Juliun's nausea. When Juliun got up out of the wheelchair, he hugged and thanked the nurse. I followed Juliun's example and did the same. The nurse and I then helped Juliun into the car, entering the car only required one step from the wheelchair.

As I helped Juliun put on his seatbelt, he started vomiting. He asked me to keep the car still. I put my hazard lights on and comforted Juliun as much as I could while he vomited. Juliun had not had anything to eat or drink for nearly 24 hours, yet he kept vomiting. He was vomiting fluid, which I guess was the anesthetics and intravenous medications. I was concerned that he would get dehydrated, and I asked him if I could take him to the hospital. Juliun paused, I think he thought seriously about this, and then said he wanted to go home.

I drove slowly and prayed intensely. Juliun needed immediate blessings. I asked God to please bless Juliun with everything that he needed. When we arrived home, there were two young men from our church who came to help Juliun get up the stairs and into our house. The young men were very sensitive to Juliun's state, and I know they wanted to respect his dignity as much as possible. Juliun wanted to try and hop without assistance. The young men respected his wishes and followed closely behind. Juliun hopped on his left foot from the car to the stairs, and then he hopped up the flight of stairs without any help. When he entered the front door, he sat down, as he felt very weak, lightheaded, and nauseous. The young men praised Juliun for his strength, and we thanked them for coming to help.

Juliun wanted to be as independent as he could, and he did not want to create extra work or worry for me. During this unforgettable and very tender evening, Juliun accepted that he was going to need help at this particular time. I was happy to do everything I could to help my son, who had one working leg and one working arm, yet I knew it was best for him to do as much as he could by himself. This required deep thinking and lots of creativity. I never really understood how important our hands were, or how much we use both hands simultaneously to do most tasks.

Despite Juliun's discomfort, thirst, fatigue, and everything else he was feeling, he did not want to drink, eat, or take pain medicine because he did not want to throw up again. Juliun did throw up a few more times before he finally fell asleep. He had pillows all around him to help him be as comfortable as possible. His arm and leg needed ice packs and elevation; we did our best to have his limbs in the correct position, and the ice packs where they needed to be. I laid down close to the door and rested with one eye and both ears open.

Juliun had night sweats and extremely intense dreams during the night, which we believe were caused by the abundance of medication he was given before, during, and after surgery. His dreams were vivid and mind-blowing. Juliun had never experienced out-of-body illusions like this before, and he didn't know what to make of them when they were happening. We were both very grateful when morning came and this night was behind us.

Within a few days, Juliun was able to use his right leg and foot. When we unwrapped his leg bandages to clean his wounds and put new bandages on, we saw the incisions in his leg for the first time. There were ten slits going down the back of his calf measuring 1 ½ to 2 inches long. The horizontal slits started about three inches below the back of his knee and were spaced about one inch apart; they ended right by his Achilles tendon. There was also one vertical slit next to his right ankle bone. Each slit had several stitches, and they all looked like they were healing well. We were grateful for this blessing.

Juliun had weekly appointments with the orthopedic surgeon; we were always happy to see him, and we truly believed that the doctor felt the same way about us. Nine days after surgery, Juliun had his leg stitches removed. On November 26, Juliun's cast was briefly taken off so that his arm stitches could be taken out. When his arm was free of stitches, Juliun asked the doctor if he could wash his arm with soap and water. As he stood at the sink with water running on his arm, he smiled. It had been 16 days since he last washed his arm, and it felt awesome. The water splashing on his numb arm also felt strange, as he had some surprising sensations that he hadn't felt for over two months; this was exciting.

The doctor then put another cast on Juliun's arm; this one was a bit smaller. During this visit and the previous two visits, the doctor asked about the pain Juliun experienced. Juliun shared that he was experiencing minimal pain, and he had not needed to take any prescription pain medication. The doctor was totally shocked by this statement. We were so grateful for this, and we knew where this blessing was coming from.

I frequently got emotional at these appointments. As I sat in the exam rooms with Juliun and listened to the doctor share his thoughts, tears of gratitude filled my spirit and eyes. So much had happened, so many people had helped, and so many blessings had been poured down on us. Because this was an emergency situation, we did not get to pick our doctors. Juliun and I both felt so grateful for the doctors who were on duty and for the doctors who were still helping him heal. I again realized that doctors were partners with God in helping people get well.

Chapter 14: Special Days

Friday, November 30th, was a special day for Juliun and his heroes. The Big Wave Risk Assessment Group Annual Summit (BWRAG) took place at Turtle Bay Hilton. BWRAG's mission is to educate and train surfers in ocean safety. On this memorable day, at this event, Juliun's champions received public recognition for their heroic rescue that saved his life. Jesse, Drew, Flynn, Ryan, Jose, and Bret were given the Palapala Ho'ohanohano Waterman Award. This honor certificate expresses even more than high status and respect, it also includes the word Waterman. The word Waterman in the surfing world is a very powerful word. To call a surfer a Waterman is extremely special.

During the award ceremony, each hero shared his thoughts about the events of September 8th. Juliun spoke first. His comments were full of gratitude and emotion for the amazing men, who were once again in his presence. The microphone was then passed down the line for the six brave, selfless men to share their thoughts. There was a clear and definite theme present in each speech. The heroes all acknowledged divine intervention; they knew they were meant to be surfing at this precise location at this exact moment. They all knew that they needed to help and rescue a fellow surfer who had just been bitten by a shark. The heroes recognized the power of their teamwork. Each courageous hero also complimented Juliun on his strength, calmness, and sustained sense of gratitude. These six stalwart men did what they did, without hesitation or thoughts of self-preservation, because they saw a young man who desperately needed help. Bret, Ryan, Drew, Jesse, Flynn, and Jose saved Juliun's life, and we will be forever grateful to each of them. Heroes are real and when you see someone in need, help them.

After the summit, Juliun felt a warm pulsing in his thumb that lasted a few minutes. When you have experienced trauma and have suffered extensive injuries, every step forward in the healing process is a joyous milestone. Every time Juliun felt something new or was able to do something he hadn't done since the shark bite, we celebrated. We felt so incredibly grateful and hopeful.

Tuesday, December 25th was a special day. On this beautiful Christmas afternoon, Juliun gave himself the gift of surfing. Yes, Juliun returned to the ocean to do what he loves. The cast that he had worn for five weeks and six days had been removed on Friday, and he was now wearing a plastic brace that could get wet. As I stood on the beach watching him surf, I burst with emotion. I was so grateful for all the blessings and miracles that had gotten him to this point. I was also grateful that he did not let his fear of sharks stop him from doing what brings him so much joy. And, as I have mentioned previously, I did what I do so well, I worried.

Monday, June 17th was a special day. At the start of our 3:45 p.m. doctors appointment, Juliun stood and used his right hand to shake the orthopedic surgeons hand as he entered the exam room. Every handshake up until this time had been with Juliun's left hand; this was the first time Juliun shook his doctor's hand. This was a happy day.

55

Monday, August 12th was a special day. Juliun spoke to a large class of fourth graders about his shark attack. Juliun started his speech by asking the children a few questions: Do you like sharks? Do you like surfing? Have you ever been bitten by a shark? Juliun then shared a child friendly version of his story and invited the children to ask questions. Juliun seemed so comfortable and confident with the children. It was beautiful to witness Juliun touching the lives of these wonderful children. The children expressed their gratitude by creating lovely, colorful thank you cards, which Juliun received on August 22nd.

These are only a handful of special days that we have had. As I looked back in my journal, in order to share these highlights with you, I felt happy reflecting on these special days. In addition, I was grateful for the inspiration that prompted me to start documenting this journey on the day that Juliun was bitten. When we look for the blessings in our lives, every day is a special day!

Chapter 15: Miracles and Blessings

Juliun and I wanted to include a chapter where we could list (we called it *Blast*) as many of the miracles and blessings that we remembered, and for which we are so grateful. Most of the sentences or phrases are concise in order to get right to the point. As you read through this lengthy list, we hope you will feel the spirit of our deep gratitude.

We are so grateful for these miracles and blessings:

- Juliun is alive.

- Juliun is healthy and strong.

- Hurricane Olivia's swell that attracted the heroes to surf this spot.

- The shark did not attack in the first 100 minutes of Juliun being in the water because the men he needed to save and rescue him were not in proximity at this time.

- Juliun did not see the shark before it bit him.

- Juliun's arms and hands were on his board.

- The shark did not bite his leg.

- The shark did not bite his body/trunk.

- The shark did not remove his arm.

- The shark let go.

- The shark did not pull him under the water.

- The shark did not knock him off his surfboard.

- The shark did not bite again.

- The shark did not attack anyone else.

- The shark did not come back.

- Additional sharks did not come.

- Juliun was able to yell for help and warn others of the shark.

- Juliun was able to paddle with both arms for a short period.

- Juliun stayed calm.

- Juliun did not lose consciousness.

- Juliun was able to hold his breath when the big wave hit him.

- The big wave came; it helped separate Juliun from the shark, and it also dispersed the blood that was in the water.

- Juliun resurfaced after being tossed around underwater.

- Juliun was able to call for help again.

- Timing of each event, especially in regards to the heroes.

- Timing of each and every miraculous detail.

- Angels.

- The heroes saw and heard Juliun.

- The heroes went to Juliun's rescue.

- The heroes knew first aid, and they knew how to apply a tourniquet.

- Surf leashes that were used for tourniquets.

- Tourniquets were administered immediately.

- The ocean was calmed shortly after the attack.

- Mitchell retrieved Juliun's lost surfboard; this board played an important part in getting Juliun to shore quickly.

- The heroes were able to get Juliun to shore in record time (about 7 minutes). The normal paddle time is 20+ minutes.

- Noah and Tiffany had just put stairs in on their shoreline.

- Surfers.

- Power of God.

- Flynn's clamping Juliun's artery.

- Feelings of peace.

- Feelings of comfort.

- Feelings of assurance.

- Ambulances and skilled paramedics.

- Fast, safe ambulance ride to Queen's.

- Hospital's Fully Activated Trauma Team was in place and ready to take care of Juliun.

- Universities that trained the doctors and nurses.

- Doctors and nurses dedication and years of hard work.

- Juliun did not need a blood transfusion.

- Juliun's arteries were not torn by the shark.

- Juliun's bones were not broken.

- Juliun's joints were not damaged.

- Juliun had adequate blood flow to his hand.

- Juliun had sensation in the palm side of his hand.

- Juliun was able to move his fingers a little.

- Juliun's elbow and bicep are strong.

- Juliun did not have a pseudoaneurysm.

- The powerful prayers from family, friends, and strangers.

- Feeling the prayers offered in our behalf.

- Juliun's pain was manageable.

- Juliun did not need strong prescription pain medicine.

- Juliun's attitude is outstanding and positive.

- Juliun is full of gratitude.

- Juliun is sleeping well.

- Employment and our wonderful employers.

- Support from employers and co-workers.

- Family and friends seeing the miracles and blessings.

- Health insurance.

- The strength of every person who has been attacked by a shark.

- The love and support given to shark victims and their families.

- People who show love and kindness to those in need.

- Phone call from Jamie, a famous surfer, that gave Juliun a big boost.

- Prayer is available 24/7.

- Fasting.

- Promptings.

- Revelation.

- The invention of surfing.

- Beautiful island of Oahu that I call home.

- Surfing buddies.

- There were a lot of surfers in the ocean.

- Helping hands.

- Selflessness of others.

- Skill set of heroes.

- Peace of mind.

- Emergency personnel were notified immediately.

- Ambulance arrived shortly after I got to shore.

- Hospitality of neighbors that allowed me to use their property.

- Strength and stamina of surfers who pushed me in.

- Leadership in the midst of terror.

- Calmness and comfort that came over me when the heroes arrived.

- Overwhelming comfort I felt when I was being rescued.

- Assurance from others.

- Encouraging words, love, and support from bystanders.

- Gratitude I felt.

- Importance of saying thanks.

- Sense of relief.

- I did not go into shock until I was in the care of medical experts.

- Bleeding was controlled with two surf leashes and axillary artery being clamped.

- Teamwork.

- Power of unity.

- Had the strength to walk.

- The towels that were used to suppress my bleeding.

- Being watched by a young mother who had medical training.

- The gift of speech.

- Expertise of paramedics.

- Therapy and Therapists.

- IVs.

- Got to the hospital in record time; normal driving time is 60+ minutes.

- I was able to keep my whole arm.

- Medical equipment.

- Minimal to no nerve pain.

- Every milestone.

- Man who told his son to call 911.

- Three women who called 911.

- Balloons and get well cards.

- Temples and Temple Prayer Rolls.

- Rainbows.

- Tender mercies.

- Feeling God's love.

- Feeling our Savior's love.

- Miracles.

- Friends sharing miraculous stories with us.

- Dreams of being healed.

- Scriptures.

- Deep breaths.

- Birds singing.

- Missions and Missionaries.

- Handshakes.

- Seeing the healing and recovery of friends.

- Mitchell creating a Go Fund Me.

- Lomilomi massages.

- Chiropractic care.

- Empathy.

- I knew I was going to be okay, I had a sense of certainty that I was going to make it.

Chapter 16: One Day At A Time

"One Day At A Time" is a phrase I have heard throughout my life. Whenever I have heard this, it has usually come from someone who was going through a hardship. I never really understood what this meant until now. There have been times during this ordeal when I felt I needed to break this down even more, maybe even one minute at a time. This would happen when the worry would consume me. It would happen when I was not focused on all of the miracles that we had been blessed with. It would happen when I was exhausted. It would also happen when I felt overwhelmed and powerless. In other words, this would happen when I was not being strong, calm, and grateful.

This extremely rare and still hard-to-accept incident has been filled with ups, downs, joy, sorrow, comfort, pain, bravery, fear, growth, love, peace, empathy, faith, appreciation, respect, patience, strength, calmness, and gratefulness. Being bitten on the arm by a shark and sustaining the injuries that resulted from this, have been a life-changing experience. Juliun and I have felt a deeper level of strong emotions, and we have learned powerful lessons that we would not have learned otherwise. As you can probably guess, one of the strongest emotions we have felt is gratitude, and for this we are grateful.

I recently heard someone say, "We all need each other." This comment resonated with me because it is so true. We all have strengths, interests, passions, and things we do well. There are times in life when we need help from others who have expertise and skills that we don't have, like a doctor. I am so grateful for those who have worked so hard and

for so long to cultivate, strengthen, and master a skill that is used to help and bless the

lives of others.

Chapter 17: Aloha and Mahalo

Juliun continues to improve a little each day. His wrist, hand, and fingers have a limited range of motion, and part of his arm and hand are still numb. On days when we feel a little sad or impatient, we remind ourselves that nerves heal very slowly (one millimeter each day, which is about one inch per month). We also know that about seventy percent of the muscle has to be innervated before it fires, and then as you get closer to 100%, it gets stronger and stronger and stronger. As Juliun's nerve continues to heal, we have faith that he will have full use, function, and sensation in the areas where he was injured.

In Hawaiian the word Aloha has several meanings, the greatest of which is Love. As we finish our story, we want to express our love to Heavenly Father, Jesus Christ, our family, friends, and everyone who has been bitten by a shark. You, the readers of this book, are our friends. Throughout this journey, we have strengthened our relationships and been so blessed to make new friends.

When you say the word Mahalo, you are expressing your gratitude and saying *Thank You.* Our hearts are so full of gratitude for every miracle, every blessing, and every answered prayer. We are truly grateful to God, Flynn, Jesse, Bret, Jose, Drew, Ryan, Mitchell, the paramedics, the doctors and nurses at Queen's Hospital, the Orthopedic Surgeon, the Anesthesiologist, the Hand Therapists, the Chiropractor, our family, and all of our friends for everything they have done to help us during this season of our life.

As I shared in Chapter 1, it is our sincere hope that this story will be a comfort and strength to those in need throughout the world. We wrote this story for you, and we pray that you will always remember these five things:

1. God is near.

2. Miracles happen.

3. Heroes are real.

4. When you see someone in need, help them.

5. Be Strong, Calm, and Grateful.

References

Edmonds, Molly. "How Tiger Sharks Work." *HowStuffWorks*, 28 Apr. 2008,

    https://animals.howstuffworks.com/fish/sharks/tiger-shark1.htm

Handwerk, Brian. "Shark Facts: Attack Stats, Record Swims, More." *National*

    Geographic, 15 Aug. 2018, www.nationalgeographic.com/animals/2005/06/shark-

    facts/

"Tiger Shark." *National Geographic*, 21 Sept. 2018,

    www.nationalgeographic.com/animals/fish/t/tiger-shark/

☺☺ Contact Email: healingwithasmile2018@gmail.com

www.ingramcontent.com/pod-product-compliance
Lightning Source LLC
Chambersburg PA
CBHW081012040426
42443CB00016B/3491